Collins

KS1
Arithmetic
SATs Question Book

Tom Hall

Contents

Addition and Subtraction

Multiplication and Division

Fractions

- You will need a pen or pencil and an eraser.

- You may not use a calculator or a ruler to answer any of the questions.

- Show your working in the space or on the grids provided.

- All answers are worth 1 mark.

- Where questions are expressed as fractions, the answers should be given as fractions. All other answers should be given as whole numbers.

- There are three progress tests throughout the book to allow you to practise the skills again. Record your results in the progress charts to identify what you are doing well in and what you can improve.

ACKNOWLEDGEMENTS

The author and publisher are grateful to the copyright holders for permission to use quoted materials and images.

Every effort has been made to trace copyright holders and obtain their permission for the use of copyright material.
The author and publisher will gladly receive information enabling them to rectify any error or omission in subsequent editions.
All facts are correct at time of going to press.

Published by Collins
An imprint of HarperCollinsPublishers Ltd
1 London Bridge Street
London SE1 9GF

HarperCollinsPublishers
1st Floor, Watermarque Building, Ringsend Road, Dublin 4, Ireland

© HarperCollinsPublishers Limited 2022

ISBN 9780008253158

First published 2017
This edition published 2022

10 9

British Library Cataloguing in Publication Data.

A CIP record of this book is available from the British Library.

Author: Tom Hall
Commissioning Editors: Michelle I'Anson and Rebecca Skinner
Editor: Katie Galloway
Project Managers: Rebecca Skinner and Katie Galloway
Cover Design: Sarah Duxbury and Kevin Robbins
Inside Concept Design: Paul Oates
Text Design and Layout: Contentra Technologies
Production: Natalia Rebow
Printed in the UK, by Martins The Printers

MIX
Paper from
responsible source

FSC
www.fsc.org
FSC™ C007454

This book is produced from independently certified FSC™ paper to ensure responsible forest management.

For more information visit:
www.harpercollins.co.uk/green

1 More, 1 Less

1   7 + 1 = 8

            1 mark

2   15 + 1 = 16

            1 mark

3   10 – 1 = 9

            1 mark

4   20 – 1 = 19

            1 mark

5   29 + 1 = 30

            1 mark

6   31 – 1 = 30

            1 mark

4   **Total marks .... /6**   **How am I doing?** 😊 😐

1   5 + 3 = $\boxed{8}$

1 mark

2   4 − 2 = $\boxed{2}$

1 mark

3   4 + 4 = $\boxed{8}$

1 mark

4   9 − 3 = $\boxed{6}$

1 mark

5   5 + 6 = $\boxed{11}$

1 mark

6   11 − 4 = $\boxed{7}$

1 mark

7 $9 + 5 = \boxed{14}$

1 mark

8 $14 - 6 = \boxed{}$

1 mark

9 $9 + 0 = \boxed{9}$

1 mark

10 $\boxed{6} = 8 - 8$

1 mark

11 $\boxed{} = 7 + 10$

12 $13 - 4 = \boxed{}$

1 mark

6

13 $0 + 0 =$ [0]

1 mark

14 $10 + 10 =$ [20]

1 mark

15 [ ] $= 10 + 7$

1 mark

16 $20 - 8 =$ [ ]

1 mark

17 $8 + 9 =$ [ ]

1 mark

18 [ ] $= 19 - 5$

1 mark

Total marks .... /18   How am I doing? 🙂 😐 😣

Add Three 1-Digit Numbers

1 $3 + 3 + 2 = \boxed{8}$

1 mark

2 $5 + 1 + 3 = \boxed{}$

1 mark

3 $5 + 5 + 0 = \boxed{10}$

1 mark

4 $2 + 6 + 6 = \boxed{}$

1 mark

5 $\boxed{} = 4 + 3 + 5$

1 mark

6 $7 + 1 + 4 = \boxed{}$

1 mark

7   4 + 6 + 8 = [ ]

1 mark

8   6 + 5 + 8 = [ ]

1 mark

9   7 + 7 + 6 = [ ]

10   [ ] = 9 + 3 + 6

1 mark

1 mark

11   8 + 8 + 7 = [ ]

12   7 + 8 + 9 = [ ]

1 mark

1 mark

Total marks .... /12   How am I doing?

1 21 + 7 = ⬚

1 mark

2 45 + 3 = ⬚

1 mark

3 ⬚ = 61 + 4

1 mark

4 ⬚ = 32 + 7

1 mark

5 60 + 8 = ⬚

1 mark

6 ⬚ = 45 + 0

1 mark

7   27 − 2 = ☐

1 mark

8   38 − 4 = ☐

1 mark

9   ☐ = 39 − 7

1 mark

10   ☐ = 54 − 4

1 mark

11   88 − 0 = 88

1 mark

12   ☐ = 67 − 5

1 mark

Add and Subtract 2-Digit Numbers and Ones

13   28 + 4 = ☐

1 mark

14   37 + 3 = 39

1 mark

15   ☐ = 46 + 6

1 mark

16   ☐ = 55 + 7

1 mark

17   7 + 58 = ☐

1 mark

18   ☐ = 9 + 72

1 mark

19 30 − 7 = [   ]

1 mark

20 42 − 5 = [   ]

1 mark

21 [   ] = 73 − 8

1 mark

22 [   ] = 77 − 9

1 mark

23 43 − 6 = [   ]

1 mark

24 [   ] = 74 − 8

1 mark

25 21 − 6 = ☐

1 mark

26 34 + 8 = ☐

1 mark

27 ☐ = 9 + 48

1 mark

28 ☐ = 63 − 6

1 mark

29 35 − 8 = ☐

1 mark

30 ☐ = 84 + 7

1 mark

Total marks .... /30   How am I doing?

1 20 + 20 = ☐

1 mark

2 30 − 20 = ☐

1 mark

3 ☐ = 50 − 10

1 mark

4 ☐ = 60 − 30

1 mark

5 30 + 30 = ☐

1 mark

6 ☐ = 50 + 20

1 mark

Add and Subtract Tens

7   60 + 10 = [ ]

1 mark

8   60 − 20 = [ ]

1 mark

9   [ ] = 30 + 40

1 mark

10   [ ] = 70 − 30

1 mark

11   40 − 40 = [ ]

1 mark

12   [ ] = 60 + 30

1 mark

13 20 + 20 + 10 = ☐

I mark ◯

14 50 + 20 + 10 = ☐

I mark ◯

15 ☐ = 40 + 10 + 30

I mark ◯

16 ☐ = 50 + 10 + 10

I mark ◯

17 10 + 30 + 30 = ☐

I mark ◯

18 ☐ = 40 + 20 + 40

I mark ◯

Total marks .... /18

How am I doing? 😊 😐 😣

1   12 + 10 = ☐

1 mark

2   29 + 20 = ☐

1 mark

3   ☐ = 35 + 20

1 mark

4   ☐ = 54 + 30

1 mark

5   30 + 47 = ☐

1 mark

6   30 + 61 = ☐

1 mark

7 | 32 − 10 = [   ]

1 mark

8 | 45 − 20 = [   ]

1 mark

9 | [   ] = 58 − 40

10 | [   ] = 76 − 10

1 mark

11 | 68 − 30 = [   ]

12 | [   ] = 88 − 70

1 mark

13 | 15 + 40 = ⬚

1 mark

14 | 34 − 20 = ⬚

1 mark

15 | ⬚ = 48 + 30

1 mark

16 | ⬚ = 20 + 71

1 mark

17 | 68 − 40 = ⬚

18 | ⬚ = 91 − 70

1 mark

1 mark

19 38 + 40 = ⬚

1 mark

20 96 − 80 = ⬚

1 mark

21 ⬚ = 85 − 80

1 mark

22 ⬚ = 78 − 30

1 mark

23 60 + 47 = ⬚

1 mark

24 ⬚ = 12 + 90

1 mark

Add and Subtract Two 2-Digit Numbers

1   16 + 22 = ☐

1 mark

2   36 + 31 = ☐

1 mark

3   ☐ = 22 + 41

1 mark

4   ☐ = 25 + 33

1 mark

5   43 + 24 = ☐

1 mark

6   ☐ = 58 + 12

1 mark

7 37 − 26 = ☐

1 mark

8 66 − 51 = ☐

1 mark

9 ☐ = 45 − 24

1 mark

10 ☐ = 65 − 45

1 mark

11 66 − 43 = ☐

12 ☐ = 31 − 28

1 mark

13 32 + 26 = ☐

1 mark

14 47 − 16 = ☐

1 mark

15 ☐ = 47 + 22

16 ☐ = 68 − 47

1 mark

1 mark

17 41 + 28 = ☐

18 ☐ = 65 − 25

1 mark

1 mark

19 31 − 12 = ⬚

1 mark

20 22 + 38 = ⬚

1 mark

21 ⬚ = 44 + 28

1 mark

22 ⬚ = 75 − 68

1 mark

23 62 − 27 = ⬚

1 mark

24 ⬚ = 68 + 23

1 mark

25 54 − 27 = [ ]

1 mark

26 48 + 43 = [ ]

1 mark

27 [ ] = 84 − 68

1 mark

28 [ ] = 36 + 77

1 mark

29 54 + 58 = [ ]

1 mark

30 [ ] = 85 − 37

1 mark

Total marks .... /30

How am I doing?

1 26 + 1 = [27]

1 mark

2 [ ] = 13 + 7

1 mark

3 76 − 8 = [ ]

1 mark

4 67 − 40 = [ ]

1 mark

5 3 + 6 + 5 = [ ]

1 mark

6 [ ] = 50 + 10 + 30

1 mark

7 33 + 60 = ☐

1 mark

8 83 − 8 = ☐

1 mark

9 45 + 53 = ☐

10 76 − 48 = ☐

1 mark

1 mark

11 26 + 56 = ☐

12 ☐ = 73 − 39

1 mark

1 mark

Total marks .... /12   How am I doing?

Question	Requirement	Mark
Page 4 1 More, 1 Less		
1	8	1
2	16	1
3	9	1
4	19	1
5	30	1
6	30	1
Pages 5–7 Add and Subtract within and to 20		
1	8	1
2	2	1
3	8	1
4	6	1
5	11	1
6	7	1
7	14	1
8	8	1
9	9	1
10	0	1
11	17	1
12	9	1
13	0	1
14	20	1
15	17	1
16	12	1
17	17	1
18	14	1
Pages 8–9 Add Three 1-Digit Numbers		
1	8	1
2	9	1
3	10	1
4	14	1
5	12	1

Question	Requirement	Mark
6	12	1
7	18	1
8	19	1
9	20	1
10	18	1
11	23	1
12	24	1
Pages 10–14 Add and Subtract 2-Digit Numbers and Ones		
1	28	1
2	48	1
3	65	1
4	39	1
5	68	1
6	45	1
7	25	1
8	34	1
9	32	1
10	50	1
11	88	1
12	62	1
13	32	1
14	40	1
15	52	1
16	62	1
17	65	1
18	81	1
19	23	1
20	37	1
21	65	1
22	68	1
23	37	1

Answers

Question	Requirement	Mark
24	66	I
25	15	I
26	42	I
27	57	I
28	57	I
29	27	I
30	91	I
Pages 15–17 Add and Subtract Tens		
I	40	I
2	10	I
3	40	I
4	30	I
5	60	I
6	70	I
7	70	I
8	40	I
9	70	I
10	40	I
11	0	I
12	90	I
13	50	I
14	80	I
15	80	I
16	70	I
17	70	I
18	100	I
Pages 18–21 Add and Subtract 2-Digit Numbers and Tens		
I	22	I
2	49	I
3	55	I
4	84	I

Question	Requirement	Mark
5	77	I
6	91	I
7	22	I
8	25	I
9	18	I
10	66	I
11	38	I
12	18	I
13	55	I
14	14	I
15	78	I
16	91	I
17	28	I
18	21	I
19	78	I
20	16	I
21	5	I
22	48	I
23	107	I
24	102	I
Pages 22–26 Add and Subtract Two 2-Digit Numbers		
I	38	I
2	67	I
3	63	I
4	58	I
5	67	I
6	70	I
7	11	I
8	15	I
9	21	I
10	20	I
11	23	I

Answers

Question	Requirement	Mark
12	3	1
13	58	1
14	31	1
15	69	1
16	21	1
17	69	1
18	40	1
19	19	1
20	60	1
21	72	1
22	7	1
23	35	1
24	91	1
25	27	1
26	91	1
27	16	1
28	113	1
29	112	1
30	48	1
Pages 27–28 Progress Test 1		
1	27	1
2	20	1
3	68	1
4	27	1
5	14	1
6	90	1
7	93	1
8	75	1
9	98	1
10	28	1
11	82	1
12	34	1

Question	Requirement	Mark
Pages 29–30 Missing Number Problems		
1	2	1
2	10	1
3	19	1
4	0	1
5	4	1
6	25	1
7	20	1
8	82	1
9	72	1
10	48	1
11	46	1
12	32	1
Pages 31–32 Addition		
1	6	1
2	4	1
3	0	1
4	7	1
5	9	1
6	6	1
7	12	1
8	17	1
9	37	1
10	11	1
11	56	1
12	67	1
Pages 33–35 Multiplication and Division Facts for 2		
1	10	1
2	14	1
3	8	1
4	22	1
5	4	1

Answers

Question	Requirement	Mark
6	16	1
7	3	1
8	6	1
9	1	1
10	12	1
11	9	1
12	10	1
13	0	1
14	24	1
15	2	1
16	14	1
17	9	1
18	8	1
Pages 36–38 Multiplication and Division Facts for 5		
1	15	1
2	30	1
3	40	1
4	55	1
5	20	1
6	60	1
7	10	1
8	5	1
9	7	1
10	2	1
11	9	1
12	1	1
13	11	1
14	45	1
15	5	1
16	60	1
17	4	1
18	30	1

Question	Requirement	Mark
Pages 39–42 Multiplication and Division Facts for 10		
1	20	1
2	60	1
3	0	1
4	100	1
5	40	1
6	110	1
7	3	1
8	1	1
9	7	1
10	12	1
11	5	1
12	9	1
13	8	1
14	10	1
15	10	1
16	60	1
17	12	1
18	90	1
Pages 42–43 Progress Test 2		
1	37	1
2	83	1
3	65	1
4	42	1
5	29	1
6	86	1
7	15	1
8	15	1
9	45	1
10	11	1
11	10	1
12	20	1

Question	Requirement	Mark
Pages 44–46 Halves		
1	4	1
2	5	1
3	7	1
4	1	1
5	10	1
6	9	1
7	3	1
8	12	1
9	20	1
10	8	1
11	11	1
12	15	1
13	0	1
14	6	1
15	8	1
16	20	1
17	10	1
18	1	1
Pages 47–49 Quarters		
1	1	1
2	3	1
3	5	1
4	2	1
5	4	1
6	6	1
7	10	1
8	11	1
9	0	1
10	$\frac{1}{4}$	1
11	2	1
12	20	1

Question	Requirement	Mark
13	0	1
14	4	1
15	12	1
16	8	1
17	20	1
18	40	1
Pages 50–52 Fractions		
1	2	1
2	4	1
3	$\frac{1}{3}$	1
4	3	1
5	5	1
6	10	1
7	2	1
8	6	1
9	5	1
10	15	1
11	10	1
12	30	1
13	1	1
14	6	1
15	3	1
16	7	1
17	12	1
18	9	1
Pages 53–54 Halves and Quarters		
1	8	1
2	8	1
3	4	1
4	4	1
5	11	1
6	20	1

Answers

Question	Requirement	Mark
7	4	1
8	8	1
9	12	1
10	12	1
11	12	1
12	20	1
Pages 55–56 Progress Test 3		
1	72	1
2	86	1
3	73	1
4	89	1
5	14	1
6	14	1
7	10	1
8	40	1
9	8	1
10	5	1
11	15	1
12	10	1

Progress Test 1

Q	Topic	✓ or ✗	See Page(s)
1	1 More, 1 Less		4
2	Add and Subtract within and to 20		5–7
3	Add and Subtract 2-Digit Numbers and Ones		10–14
4	Add and Subtract 2-Digit Numbers and Tens		18–21
5	Add Three 1-Digit Numbers		8–9
6	Add and Subtract Tens		15–17
7	Add and Subtract 2-Digit Numbers and Tens		18–21
8	Add and Subtract 2-Digit Numbers and Ones		10–14
9	Add and Subtract Two 2-digit Numbers		22–26
10	Add and Subtract Two 2-digit Numbers		22–26
11	Add and Subtract Two 2-digit Numbers		22–26
12	Add and Subtract Two 2-digit Numbers		22–26

Progress Test 2

Q	Topic	✓ or ✗	See Page(s)
1	Add and Subtract 2-Digit Numbers and Ones		10–14
2	Add and Subtract 2-Digit Numbers and Tens		18–21
3	Add and Subtract Two 2-digit Numbers		22–26
4	Add and Subtract Two 2-digit Numbers		22–26
5	Missing Number Problems		29–30
6	Missing Number Problems		29–30
7	Add Three 1-Digit Numbers		8–9
8	Addition		31–32
9	Multiplication and Division Facts for 5		36–38
10	Multiplication and Division Facts for 2		33–35
11	Multiplication and Division Facts for 10		39–41
12	Multiplication and Division Facts for 10		39–41

Progress Test Charts

Progress Test 3

Q	Topic	✓ or X	See Page(s)
1	Add and Subtract 2-Digit Numbers and Ones		10–14
2	Add and Subtract 2-Digit Numbers and Tens		18–21
3	Add and Subtract Two 2-digit Numbers		22–26
4	Add and Subtract Two 2-digit Numbers		22–26
5	Add Three 1-Digit Numbers		8–9
6	Multiplication and Division Facts for 2		33–35
7	Multiplication and Division Facts for 10		39–41
8	Multiplication and Division Facts for 5		36–38
9	Halves		44–46
10	Fractions		50–52
11	Fractions		50–52
12	Halves and Quarters		53–54

What am I doing well in?

_____

_____

_____

_____

What do I need to improve?

_____

_____

_____

_____

1   5 − ☐ = 3

1 mark

2   ☐ − 5 = 5

1 mark

3   ☐ − 13 = 6

1 mark

4   21 − ☐ = 21

1 mark

5   31 + ☐ = 35

1 mark

6   ☐ − 0 = 25

1 mark

7   57 − [ ] = 37

1 mark

8   [ ] − 70 = 12

1 mark

9   [ ] − 34 = 38

10   76 − [ ] = 28

1 mark

1 mark

11   41 + [ ] = 87

12   [ ] + 26 = 58

1 mark

1 mark

Total marks .... /12

How am I doing?

1   3 + 6 = ☐ + 3

       1 mark

2   5 + ☐ = 4 + 5

       1 mark

3   ☐ + 1 = 1 + 0

       1 mark

4   7 + 5 = 5 + ☐

       1 mark

5   8 + ☐ = 9 + 8

       1 mark

6   10 + 6 = ☐ + 10

       1 mark

7 $23 + 12 = \boxed{} + 23$

1 mark

8 $41 + \boxed{} = 17 + 41$

1 mark

9 $37 + 51 = 51 + \boxed{}$

1 mark

10 $71 + 11 = \boxed{} + 71$

1 mark

11 $\boxed{} + 34 = 34 + 56$

1 mark

12 $53 + \boxed{} = 67 + 53$

1 mark

Total marks .... /12

How am I doing?

1 $5 \times 2 =$ ⬚

1 mark

2 $7 \times 2 =$ ⬚

1 mark

3 $4 \times 2 =$ ⬚

4 $11 \times 2 =$ ⬚

1 mark

1 mark

5 $2 \times 2 =$ ⬚

6 $8 \times 2 =$ ⬚

1 mark

1 mark

Multiplication and Division Facts for 2

7   6 ÷ 2 = ☐

1 mark

8   12 ÷ 2 = ☐

1 mark

9   2 ÷ 2 = ☐

1 mark

10   24 ÷ 2 = ☐

1 mark

11   18 ÷ 2 = ☐

1 mark

12   20 ÷ 2 = ☐

1 mark

13 [ ] $= 0 \div 2$

1 mark

14 $12 \times 2 =$ [ ]

1 mark

15 $8 \times$ [ ] $= 16$

1 mark

16 [ ] $\div 2 = 7$

1 mark

17 [ ] $\times 2 = 18$

1 mark

18 [ ] $\div 2 = 4$

1 mark

Total marks .... /18   How am I doing?   35

Multiplication and Division Facts for 5

1 3 × 5 = ☐

1 mark

2 6 × 5 = ☐

1 mark

3 8 × 5 = ☐

1 mark

4 11 × 5 = ☐

1 mark

5 ☐ = 4 × 5

1 mark

6 ☐ = 12 × 5

1 mark

7 $50 ÷ 5 =$ ⬚

1 mark

8 $25 ÷ 5 =$ ⬚

1 mark

9 $35 ÷ 5 =$ ⬚

1 mark

10 $10 ÷ 5 =$ ⬚

1 mark

11   ⬚ $= 45 ÷ 5$

1 mark

12   ⬚ $= 5 ÷ 5$

1 mark

13 ⬚ = 55 ÷ 5

○ I mark

14 9 × 5 = ⬚

○ I mark

15 7 × ⬚ = 35

○ I mark

16 ⬚ ÷ 5 = 12

○ I mark

17 ⬚ × 5 = 20

○ I mark

18 ⬚ ÷ 5 = 6

○ I mark

Total marks .... /18

How am I doing?

1 2 × 10 = ☐

1 mark

2 6 × 10 = ☐

1 mark

3 0 × 10 = ☐

1 mark

4 10 × 10 = ☐

1 mark

5 ☐ = 4 × 10

1 mark

6 ☐ = 11 × 10

1 mark

7   30 ÷ 10 = ☐

1 mark

8   10 ÷ 10 = ☐

1 mark

9   70 ÷ 10 = ☐

1 mark

10   120 ÷ 10 = ☐

1 mark

11   ☐ = 50 ÷ 10

1 mark

12   ☐ = 90 ÷ 10

1 mark

13 [ ] $= 80 \div 10$

1 mark

14 $100 \div 10 =$ [ ]

1 mark

15 $5 \times$ [ ] $= 50$

1 mark

16 [ ] $\div 10 = 6$

1 mark

17 [ ] $\times 10 = 120$

1 mark

18 [ ] $\div 10 = 9$

1 mark

Total marks .... /18   How am I doing? 😊 😐 😣   41

Progress Test 2

1 43 − 6 = [ ]

1 mark

2 53 + 30 = [ ]

1 mark

3 37 + 28 = [ ]

1 mark

4 74 − 32 = [ ]

1 mark

5 62 + [ ] = 91

1 mark

6 [ ] − 38 = 48

1 mark

42

7 | 8 + 5 + 2 = [ ]

1 mark

8 | 83 + 15 = [ ] + 83

1 mark

9 | 9 × 5 = [ ]

1 mark

10 | 22 ÷ 2 = [ ]

1 mark

11 | 7 × [ ] = 70

1 mark

12 | [ ] ÷ 2 = 10

1 mark

8½/12

1 $\frac{1}{2}$ of 8 = 4

 ✓

1 mark

2 $\frac{1}{2}$ of 10 = 6̶ 5 ½

1 mark

3 $\frac{1}{2}$ of 14 = 7 ✓

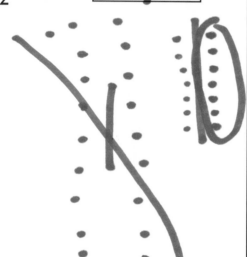

1 mark

4 $\frac{1}{2}$ of 2 = 1 ✓

1 mark

5 $\frac{1}{2}$ of 20 = 10 ✓

1 mark

6 $\frac{1}{2}$ of 18 = 9 ✓

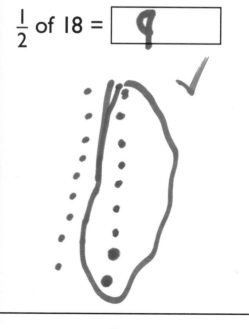

1 mark

7 | 3 | $= \frac{1}{2}$ of 6

1 mark

8 | 12 | $= \frac{1}{2}$ of 24

1 mark

9 $\frac{1}{2}$ of 40 = | 20 | ✓

10 10
10 10

1 mark

10 | 8 | $= \frac{1}{2}$ of 16 ✓

1 mark

11 | 11 | $= \frac{1}{2}$ of 22 ✓

1 mark

12 $\frac{1}{2}$ of 30 = | 10 8 | 15

10
10 10

1 mark

45

Halves

13 ☐ $= \frac{1}{2}$ of 0

1 mark

14 ☐ $= \frac{1}{2}$ of 12

1 mark

15 $\frac{1}{2}$ of ☐ $= 4$

1 mark

16 $\frac{1}{2}$ of ☐ $= 10$

1 mark

17 $5 = \frac{1}{2}$ of ☐

1 mark

18 $\frac{1}{2} = \frac{1}{2}$ of ☐

1 mark

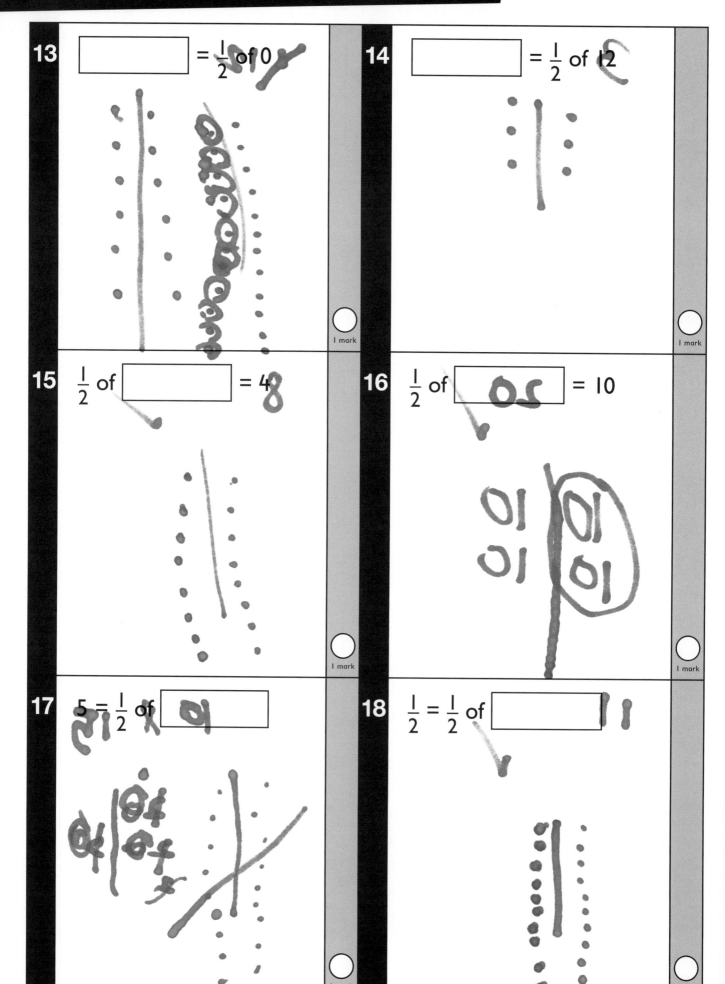

Total marks .... /18

How am I doing?

1 $\frac{1}{4}$ of 4 = ⬚

1 mark

2 $\frac{1}{4}$ of 12 = ⬚

1 mark

3 $\frac{1}{4}$ of 20 = ⬚

1 mark

4 $\frac{1}{4}$ of 8 = ⬚

1 mark

5 $\frac{1}{4}$ of 16 = ⬚

1 mark

6 $\frac{1}{4}$ of 24 = ⬚

1 mark

Quarters

7 [   ] = $\frac{1}{4}$ of 40

1 mark

8 [   ] = $\frac{1}{4}$ of 44

1 mark

9 $\frac{1}{4}$ of 0 = [   ]

1 mark

10 [   ] = $\frac{1}{4}$ of 1

1 mark

11 $\frac{1}{4}$ of 8 = [   ]

1 mark

12 $\frac{1}{4}$ of 80 = [   ]

1 mark

13 $\frac{1}{4}$ of [   ] = 0

1 mark

14 $\frac{1}{4}$ of [   ] = 1

1 mark

15 $\frac{1}{4}$ of [   ] = 3

1 mark

16 $\frac{1}{4}$ of [   ] = 2

1 mark

17 $5 = \frac{1}{4}$ of [   ]

1 mark

18 $10 = \frac{1}{4}$ of [   ]

1 mark

Total marks .... /18

How am I doing?

Fractions

1 $\frac{1}{3}$ of 6 = [   ]

2 $\frac{1}{3}$ of 12 = [   ]

3 $\frac{1}{3}$ of 1 = [   ]

4 $\frac{1}{3}$ of 9 = [   ]

5 $\frac{1}{3}$ of 15 = [   ]

6 $\frac{1}{3}$ of 30 = [   ]

7 $\frac{1}{4}$ of 8 = [ ]

8 $\frac{3}{4}$ of 8 = [ ]

9 $\frac{1}{4}$ of 20 = [ ]

10 $\frac{3}{4}$ of 20 = [ ]

11 $\frac{1}{4}$ of 40 = [ ]

12 $\frac{3}{4}$ of 40 = [ ]

Fractions

13 ⬚ $= \frac{1}{3}$ of 3

1 mark

14 ⬚ $= \frac{1}{3}$ of 18

1 mark

15 ⬚ $= \frac{3}{4}$ of 4

1 mark

16 ⬚ $= \frac{1}{3}$ of 21

1 mark

17 ⬚ $= \frac{3}{4}$ of 16

1 mark

18 ⬚ $= \frac{3}{4}$ of 12

1 mark

Total marks .... /18

How am I doing?

1 $\frac{1}{2}$ of 16 = [ ]

1 mark

2 $\frac{2}{4}$ of 16 = [ ]

1 mark

3 [ ] = $\frac{1}{2}$ of 8

1 mark

4 [ ] = $\frac{2}{4}$ of 8

1 mark

5 $\frac{2}{4}$ of 22 = [ ]

1 mark

6 $\frac{2}{4}$ of 40 = [ ]

1 mark

7 $\frac{1}{2}$ of ____ = 2

1 mark

8 $\frac{2}{4}$ of ____ = 4

1 mark

9 $\frac{1}{4}$ of ____ = 3

1 mark

10 $\frac{2}{4}$ of ____ = 6

1 mark

11 $3 = \frac{1}{4}$ of ____

1 mark

12 $10 = \frac{2}{4}$ of ____

1 mark

54

Total marks .... /12

How am I doing?

1   67 + 5= [   ]

1 mark

2   36 + 50 = [   ]

1 mark

3   45 + 28 = [   ]

1 mark

4   22 + 67 = [   ]

1 mark

5   6 + 3 + 5 = [   ]

1 mark

6   7 × 2 = [   ]

1 mark

Progress Test 3

7   20 ÷ ☐ = 2

1 mark

8   ☐ = 8 × 5

1 mark

9 $\frac{1}{2}$ of 16 = ☐

1 mark

10 $\frac{1}{3}$ of 15 = ☐

1 mark

11 $\frac{3}{4}$ of 20 = ☐

1 mark

12   ☐ = $\frac{2}{4}$ of 20

1 mark

Total marks .... /12   How am I doing? 🙂 😐 😣